Plants

Nature's RECORD-BREAKERS

Plants

Written by Antonella Meucci

Illustrated by Paola Holguín, Antonella Pastorelli, Thomas Troyer,
Andrea Morandi, Alessandro Cantucci, and Fabiano Fabbrucci

Gareth Stevens Publishing
A WORLD ALMANAC EDUCATION GROUP COMPANY

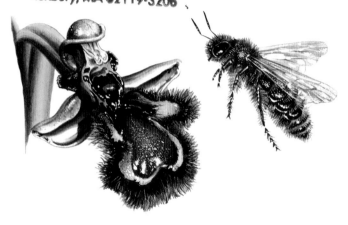

Please visit our web site at: www.garethstevens.com
For a free color catalog describing Gareth Stevens Publishing's
list of high-quality books and multimedia programs,
call 1-800-542-2595 or fax your request to (414) 332-3567.

Gareth Stevens Publishing would like to thank Neil Luebke of the Milwaukee Public Museum, Milwaukee, Wisconsin, for his kind and professional help with the information in this book.

Library of Congress Cataloging-in-Publication Data

Meucci, Antonella.
    Plants / written by Antonella Meucci; illustrated by Paola Holguín ... [et al.].
       p. cm. — (Nature's record-breakers)
    Includes bibliographical references and index.
    Summary: Discusses various types of plants, their habitats, ecosystems, and more.
    ISBN 0-8368-2908-5 (lib. bdg.)
    1. Plants—Miscellanea—Juvenile literature. [1. Plants—Miscellanea.] I. Holguín,
Paola, ill. II. Title. III. Series.
    QK49.M49   2002
    580—dc21

2001049915

This edition first published in 2002 by
Gareth Stevens Publishing
A World Almanac Education Group Company
330 West Olive Street, Suite 100
Milwaukee, Wisconsin 53212 USA

Original edition © 2000 by McRae Books Srl. First published in 2000 as *Plants and Trees*, with the series title *Blockbusters!*, by McRae Books Srl., via de' Rustici 5, Florence, Italy. This edition © 2002 by Gareth Stevens, Inc. Additional end matter © 2002 by Gareth Stevens, Inc.

Translated from Italian by Christina Longman
Designer: Marco Nardi
Layout: Ornella Fassio and Adriano Nardi
Gareth Stevens editor: Monica Rausch
Gareth Stevens designer: Scott M. Krall

Printed in the United States of America

1 2 3 4 5 6 7 8 9 06 05 04 03 02

Contents

Trees 6

Flowers 8

Fruits and Seeds 10

Herbaceous Plants 12

Carnivorous Plants and Parasites 14

Aquatic Plants 16

Desert Plants 18

Ferns, Mosses, and Horsetails 20

Fungi and Other Nonplants 22

Ecosystems 24

Unique Plants 26

Records 28

Glossary 30

Books, Videos, Web Sites 31

Index 32

Words that appear in the glossary are printed in **boldface** type
the first time they occur in the text.

Did you know?

Q. WHAT ARE TREES?

A. Trees are plants with a woody stem called a trunk. Because a tree's trunk is strong, a tree can grow very tall. Broad-leaf trees and conifers are two main types of trees.

Q. WHAT ARE CONIFERS?

A. Conifers are trees that have very narrow, needle-shaped leaves and produce cones, such as pinecones. Conifers are also called "evergreens" because most of these trees do not lose their leaves in winter. Pines, firs, cypress trees, and redwoods are all conifers.

Q. WHAT ARE BROAD-LEAF TREES?

A. Broad-leaf trees have wide, flat leaves and produce flowers and fruits. Broad-leaf trees can be either deciduous, meaning that they lose their leaves in winter, or evergreen. Oak, ash, elm, and beech trees are all broad-leaf trees.

◀ The *Ginkgo biloba*, or maidenhair tree, is the only surviving member of the Ginkgo family, a group of plants living on Earth over 160 million years ago. The tree has fan-shaped leaves that turn a beautiful bright yellow in fall.

◀ The bristlecone pine is the longest-living tree in the world. It grows in the Rocky Mountains in North America. Some bristlecone pines have reached the age of 4,900 years!

Fascinating Facts

• Plants are divided into two groups: those plants, including gymnosperms and angiosperms, that reproduce through seeds; and plants that reproduce through tiny cells called spores.

• A gymnosperm is a plant whose seeds are contained in cones. All conifers are gymnosperms.

• Angiosperms are flowering plants. Their seeds are produced by flowers and develop inside ovaries, or protective cases. Broad-leaf trees are angiosperms.

• Angiosperms appeared on Earth after gymnosperms, but now, with over 250,000 **species**, angiosperms are the most numerous group of plants.

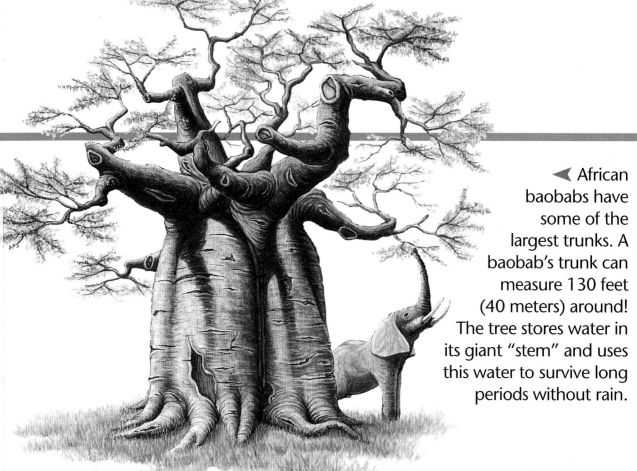

▶ African baobabs have some of the largest trunks. A baobab's trunk can measure 130 feet (40 meters) around! The tree stores water in its giant "stem" and uses this water to survive long periods without rain.

▶ Trees and other green plants, along with algae and some bacteria, are the only living **organisms** that can produce their own food. In a process called **photosynthesis**, **chlorophyll**, a substance found in plants, reacts with sunlight to change water absorbed in the plant's roots and carbon dioxide, a gas in the air, into **nutrients** and oxygen. Animals, including humans, breathe in this oxygen and breathe out the carbon dioxide plants need.

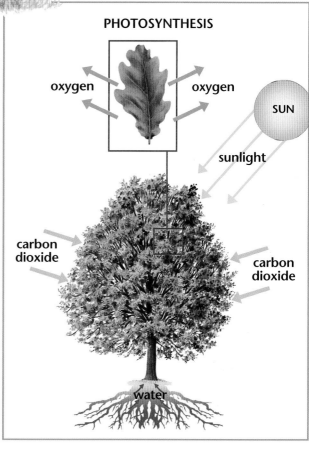

PHOTOSYNTHESIS

oxygen

oxygen

SUN

sunlight

carbon dioxide

carbon dioxide

water

Flowers

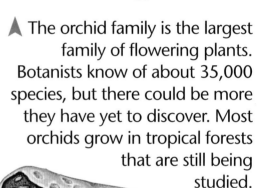

▲ A sunflower may appear to have only one big flower, but this "flower" is really a composite **inflorescence**. Lots of tiny flowers make up a sunflower's "head." This head can grow up to 30 inches (76 centimeters) wide.

▲ The orchid family is the largest family of flowering plants. Botanists know of about 35,000 species, but there could be more they have yet to discover. Most orchids grow in tropical forests that are still being studied.

► The giant rafflesia produces the largest flower in the world. Its flower can grow as big as 3 feet (1 m) in **diameter** and weigh as much as 15 pounds (7 kilograms). The huge flower, however, has a terrible smell!

▼ Magnolias are among the oldest angiosperms, or flowering plants. Fossils of these flowers date as far back as 90 million years — about 25 million years before the dinosaurs disappeared!

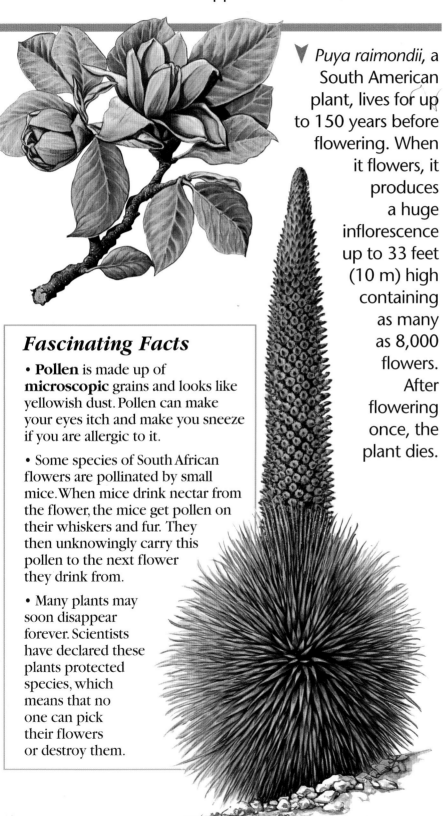

▼ *Puya raimondii*, a South American plant, lives for up to 150 years before flowering. When it flowers, it produces a huge inflorescence up to 33 feet (10 m) high containing as many as 8,000 flowers. After flowering once, the plant dies.

Fascinating Facts

• **Pollen** is made up of **microscopic** grains and looks like yellowish dust. Pollen can make your eyes itch and make you sneeze if you are allergic to it.

• Some species of South African flowers are pollinated by small mice. When mice drink nectar from the flower, the mice get pollen on their whiskers and fur. They then unknowingly carry this pollen to the next flower they drink from.

• Many plants may soon disappear forever. Scientists have declared these plants protected species, which means that no one can pick their flowers or destroy them.

Fruits and Seeds

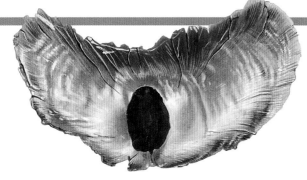

◀ Alsomitra has seeds with light, transparent wings about 6 inches (15 cm) long. The wings allow the seeds to glide long distances before they reach the ground, so the new plant will grow far away from its parent.

▼ The bird-cage plant travels a long way before dropping its seeds. This plant grows in the desert sands of California. When it dies, its stems curl up, and it forms a twisted ball. The wind rolls the plant for miles (km) over the sand. When it finds shelter from the wind, it releases its seeds.

◀ Coconuts are among the largest seeds on Earth. These seeds can weigh as much as 40 pounds (18 kg). Coconuts are covered with a special fiber that helps them float. If they fall from a coconut palm tree into water, they can float back to land.

➤ A pumpkin is actually an enormous fruit. Some pumpkins weigh over 880 pounds (400 kg).

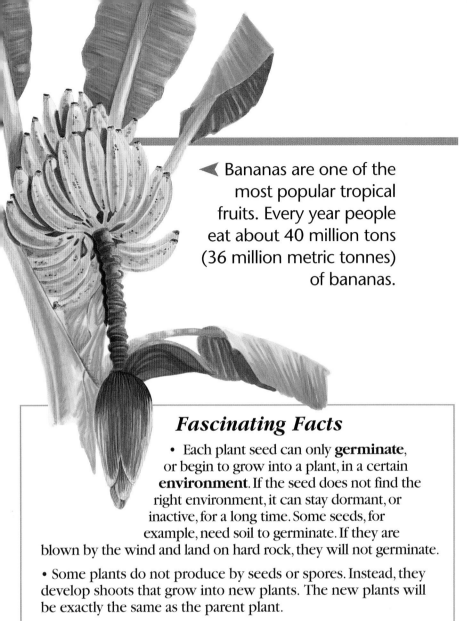

◄ Bananas are one of the most popular tropical fruits. Every year people eat about 40 million tons (36 million metric tonnes) of bananas.

Fascinating Facts

• Each plant seed can only **germinate**, or begin to grow into a plant, in a certain **environment**. If the seed does not find the right environment, it can stay dormant, or inactive, for a long time. Some seeds, for example, need soil to germinate. If they are blown by the wind and land on hard rock, they will not germinate.

• Some plants do not produce by seeds or spores. Instead, they develop shoots that grow into new plants. The new plants will be exactly the same as the parent plant.

Q. HOW DOES A FRUIT GROW?

A. After the ovules in the pistil of a flower are fertilized, the petals of the flower **wither** and fall off. Then the ovary, a structure that surrounds the ovules, grows larger and develops into a fruit.

Q. WHAT ARE SEEDS?

A. The fertilized ovules inside the fruit become seeds. Each seed contains a tiny plant, called an *embryo*, and food for that embryo. The embryo will use that food until it has developed enough to produce its own food.

Q. WHAT IS DISSEMINATION?

A. Dissemination is the process in which the seeds of a plant are scattered far away from the parent plant. Seeds need to sprout away from the parent because the parent may **deprive** the young plant of sunlight or nutrients it needs to grow. Seeds can be disseminated by wind, water, or animals.

Did you know?

Q. WHAT ARE HERBACEOUS PLANTS?

A. Herbaceous plants are plants that do not have woody stems like trees. Herbaceous plants can grow in many different environments.

Q. HOW LONG DO HERBACEOUS PLANTS LIVE?

A. Many herbaceous plants have an annual life cycle — they grow, flower, develop fruits and seeds, and die all in one year. Some herbaceous plants, however, have perennial cycles. During a cold winter, the underground parts of perennial plants stay alive after the leaves and stems die. These plants grow a new stem and leaves the following spring, and in this way, they live for several years.

Q. HOW DO PEOPLE USE HERBACEOUS PLANTS ?

A. People use herbaceous plants in clothing, food, and medicines, and in the production of a wide variety of materials.

▲ Cotton lint, the white fluff that surrounds the seeds of cotton plants, is the most widely used plant fiber in the world. People use cotton to make clothes, sheets, carpets, and many other items.

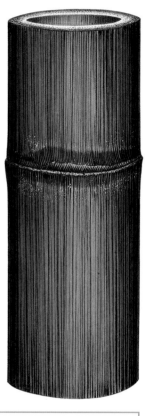

➤ Bamboos are the only members of the grass family with rigid stems. Some of the biggest species of bamboo can grow up to 130 feet (40 m) high. The stems can measure 12 inches (30 cm) in diameter.

Fascinating Facts

• Madagascar periwinkle produces a very precious substance. Doctors use this substance to treat leukemia.

• Hemp and linen are the world's oldest **textile** plants. Fibers from the stem of hemp can be made into a rough cloth or a strong rope.

• Plants specially grown for animal food are called forage. The best forage is alfalfa, which is rich in nutrients animals need.

Herbaceous Plants

➤ Stinging nettle has one of the most efficient defense systems. The leaves of this plant have hairs that break at the slightest touch, releasing an **irritating** substance. Plants such as nettle have developed defense systems so people and animals will leave them alone.

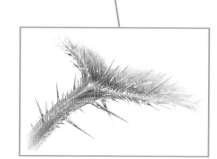

◀ Foxglove can be dangerous for humans. It produces a substance that, if taken in large **doses**, can cause the heart to beat very quickly. Doctors, however, use small doses of medicine made from foxglove to treat certain heart diseases.

➤ Wheat is the oldest and most commonly grown **cereal** in the world. Other cereals include oats, barley, rye, and rice. People have grown cereals all over the world for centuries. These plants are also some of the most important food sources for many animals.

Carnivorous Plants

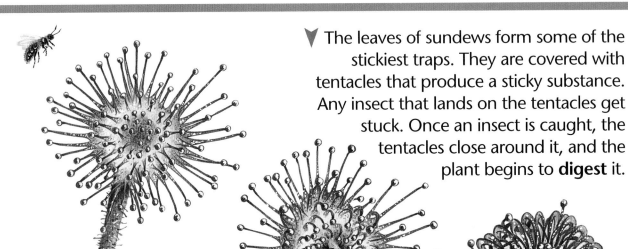

The leaves of sundews form some of the stickiest traps. They are covered with tentacles that produce a sticky substance. Any insect that lands on the tentacles get stuck. Once an insect is caught, the tentacles close around it, and the plant begins to **digest** it.

Fascinating Fact

The dodder, a parasitic climbing plant, winds itself around another plant as it grows, taking food from that plant. The dodder does not have chlorophyll, which it needs to produce its own food.

Mistletoe is a unique **parasite**. Unlike many other parasitic plants, mistletoe has chlorophyll, so it can perform photosynthesis, but it needs to absorb water and mineral salts from a **host**.

The Venus fly trap is one of only two plants that use spring traps to catch **prey**. As soon as an insect lands on the leaf of a Venus fly trap, the two sides of the leaf snap shut. The plant quickly produces special juices to digest the insect.

and Parasites

◀ The strangler fig literally strangles its host! It grows on the branches of trees (1), and its roots stretch downward until they dig into the soil. As the fig grows, it winds itself around the tree (2), robbing the tree of light and nutrients, until the tree dies. The fig, however, continues to live even after the tree has rotted away (3).

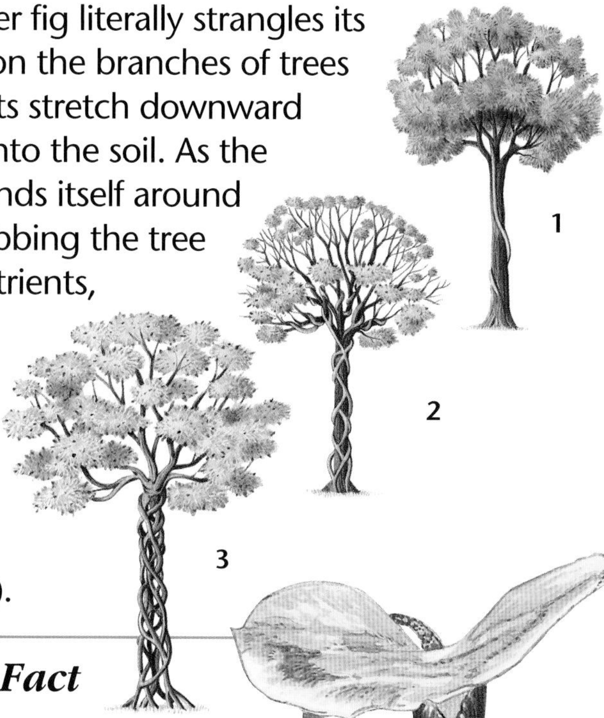

1

2

3

Fascinating Fact

The bladderwort, a water plant, uses air-filled sacs to catch prey. The sacs have tiny trap doors bordered with hairs. When an insect touches a hair, the trap door opens. As water rushes into the sac, the prey is sucked inside.

➤ The leaves of tropical pitcher plants are shaped like water pitchers. The top edges of the pitcher are coated with nectar to attract insects. Once insects are inside the pitcher, its slippery walls prevent them from climbing out. They then fall to the bottom of the pitcher where special liquids start to digest them.

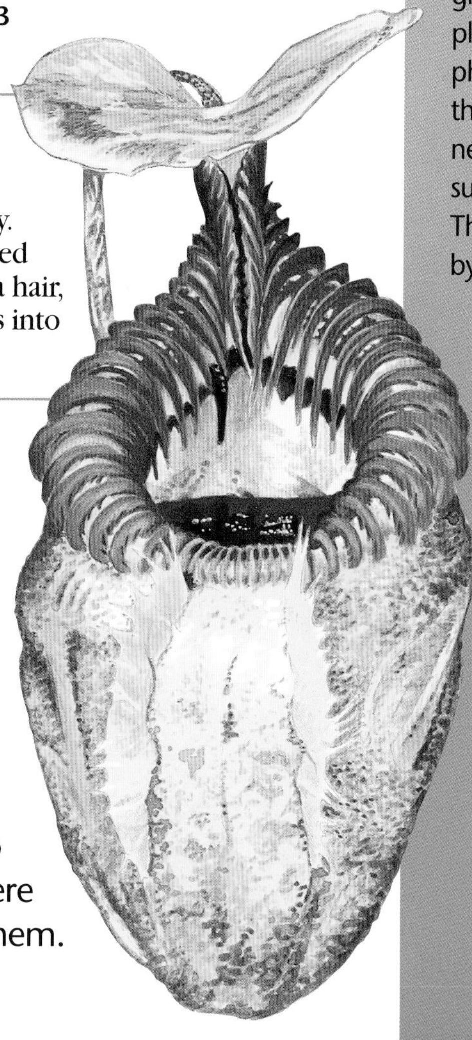

15

Aquatic

Plants

Did you know?

Q. WHAT ARE AQUATIC PLANTS?

A. Aquatic plants are plants that grow in and along bodies of water, including marshes, ponds, rivers, and oceans.

Q. HOW DO AQUATIC PLANTS LIVE?

A. Aquatic plants thrive in wet habitats. Some aquatic plants live completely underwater; some, such as water lilies, float on the water's surface; and still others can grow several yards (meters) out of the water. Some of these plants have roots anchored in the mud beneath the water, while others have free-floating roots.

Q. DO ANY PLANTS LIVE IN THE OCEAN?

A. Yes. The most common plant in the ocean is *Posidonia*, or sea grass. It grows in masses on the ocean floor, forming huge underwater meadows.

▲ Reeds, canes, rushes, and cattails are the most common plants along waterways and in ponds. Cattails have long leaves and a thick, brown inflorescence.

▲ The Egyptians used fibers from the stems of papyrus, a tall water plant, to make paper. They also made shoes, mats, and other objects out of the strong fiber. Papyrus can grow up to 16 feet (5 m) tall.

The water hyacinth, a tropical plant, is the fastest growing plant. It reproduces quickly, covering rivers, lakes, and ponds in no time. In Florida, waterways are often blocked by masses of this plant growth.

Fascinating Fact

The bald cyprus is a conifer that grows in Florida swamps. Although most of its roots are buried in the mud beneath the swamps, parts of the roots stick out above the ground. The roots need air they cannot get beneath the thick mud.

Common duckweed is the smallest known flowering plant. Its leaves measure only a few tenths of an inch (millimeters) in diameter. Each tiny leaf has its own thin root dangling beneath it in the water.

The *Victoria amazonica* is the largest lily in the world. Its floating leaves can reach over 7 feet (2 m) in diameter and can carry the weight of a six-month-old baby!

Desert Plants

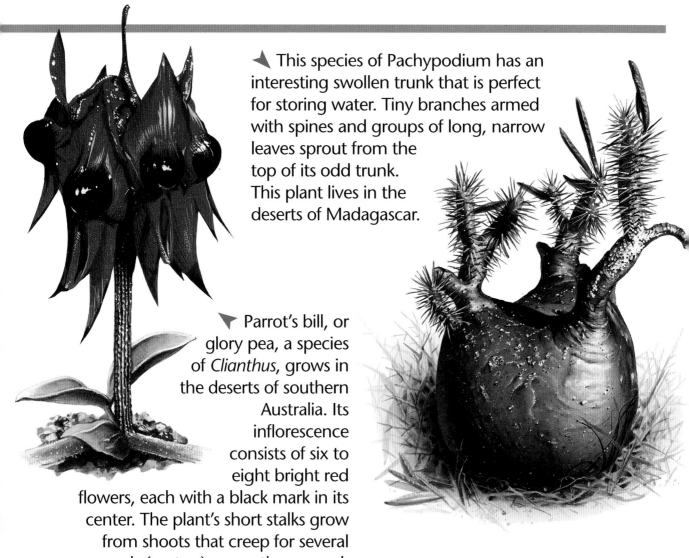

This species of Pachypodium has an interesting swollen trunk that is perfect for storing water. Tiny branches armed with spines and groups of long, narrow leaves sprout from the top of its odd trunk. This plant lives in the deserts of Madagascar.

Parrot's bill, or glory pea, a species of *Clianthus*, grows in the deserts of southern Australia. Its inflorescence consists of six to eight bright red flowers, each with a black mark in its center. The plant's short stalks grow from shoots that creep for several yards (meters) across the ground.

The Welwitschia, a plant that grows in the deserts of Namibia, can live as long as 2,000 years. It grows only two ribbonlike leaves, which split and fray, stretching up to 10 feet (3 m) over the ground.

The saguaro cactus of the Arizona desert is the biggest cactus. It can grow as high as 50 feet (15 m) and live for up to 200 years. When it rains, the cactus stores the rainwater in its stem, swelling the stem's diameter by a half.

Fascinating Facts

• Ephemeral plants are desert plants with a very short life cycle. These plants live as dormant seeds until it rains. After a rainfall, the seeds germinate, and in just a short time, the plants grow roots, flower, and die. New seeds formed by the plants are left in the ground, waiting until it rains again.

• Euphorbias grow in the African deserts and are very similar to the cacti of the Americas. Like cacti, they have spines in place of leaves.

Plants belonging to the *Lithops* genus growing in the South African deserts are sometimes called "stone plants" or "pebble plants." Only two tiny leaves on these plants stick out above ground. Because these leaves look like stones, animals that would otherwise eat the plants pass by them.

Q. HOW CAN PLANTS SURVIVE IN THE DESERT?

A. Because it rarely rains in deserts, plants that live in these areas have **adapted** special ways to gather, store, and use the little water available to them. Using these unique methods, these plants can survive long periods without rain.

Q. WHAT ARE SOME OF THE WAYS PLANTS GATHER AND STORE WATER?

A. Some plants have very long roots so they can reach water far beneath the ground. Other plants store rainwater in stems or leaves. Some plants can absorb the dew that forms on desert mornings. To avoid losing water through leaves, some plants, such as cacti, have thorns instead of leaves, and they perform photosynthesis in their green stems.

Did you know?

Q. WHAT ARE FERNS?

A. Ferns are nonflowering plants that grow in damp, dark places, such as the shade of a thick forest. About 10,000 species of ferns exist. Ferns reproduce through very light spores. Spores are similar to seeds; once spores settle in a favorable environment, they germinate, or grow into a plant.

Q. WHAT DO HORSETAILS, MOSSES, LIVERWORTS, AND FERNS HAVE IN COMMON?

A. None of these plants have flowers, and they all reproduce through spores. They are all **primitive** plants, too, and have been on Earth since prehistoric times. Mosses and liverworts, for example, appeared as far back as 425 million years ago, and Earth was once covered with forests of horsetails and gigantic ferns.

▲ Mosses make the softest living carpets! These tiny plants usually grow in damp places. They live in groups so thick that they form soft green carpets on soil or on tree trunks.

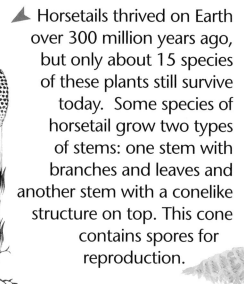

▲ Horsetails thrived on Earth over 300 million years ago, but only about 15 species of these plants still survive today. Some species of horsetail grow two types of stems: one stem with branches and leaves and another stem with a conelike structure on top. This cone contains spores for reproduction.

▶ Liverworts and mosses are the least **evolved** land plants and have the simplest structures. About 8,000 species of liverworts exist. They grow mainly in damp, moist places and get their name from their shape, which often looks like a liver.

Ferns, Mosses, and Horsetails

➤ Tree ferns are the biggest ferns. These giant plants look somewhat like palm trees. They grow in tropical regions and can be up to 60 feet (18 m) tall.

➤ New fern fronds form graceful green curls when they sprout. As the plant grows, the fronds slowly uncurl. Then they release spores from special sacs underneath the fronds, and the wind carries away the spores.

21

Fungi and Other Nonplants

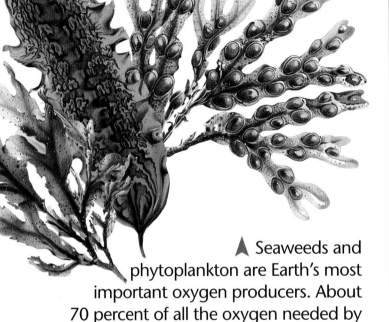

▲ Seaweeds and phytoplankton are Earth's most important oxygen producers. About 70 percent of all the oxygen needed by humans and other animals on Earth comes from the photosynthesis performed by these organisms in the ocean.

Fascinating Facts

• Although seaweeds may look like plants, they are not part of the plant kingdom. Like plants, they have chlorophyll and can perform photosynthesis, but unlike plants, seaweeds do not have roots, leaves, or stems. They also do not produce flowers or fruits. Seaweeds are a type of alga.

• Truffles are tasty mushrooms, but they are difficult to find! They grow underground in woods. Truffle gatherers use specially trained dogs and pigs to sniff out the mushrooms, since truffles have a distinct odor.

➤ The giant puffball is the biggest mushroom in the world. This mushroom can measure up to 20 inches (50 cm) in diameter and weigh as much as 40 pounds (18 kg)! The puffball is edible and grows in the forests of Europe and North America.

◀ The death cap is the most poisonous mushroom for humans. A person could die after eating it. Many other fungi are also poisonous for humans.

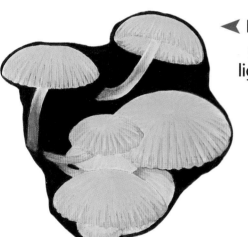

◀ Luminous mushrooms can give off a strange greenish light that can be seen up to 98 feet (30 m) away. The brightest of these luminous fungi grow in the Pacific Ocean around the Philippines.

▲ Lichens are some of the toughest organisms. They usually grow on rock, and they can live in very harsh environments where plants cannot grow. Lichens also can survive very high or low temperatures. Some types of lichens in the Antarctic, for example, can live in temperatures as low as -4° F (-20° C)!

Did you know?

Q. WHAT ARE FUNGI?

A. Fungi are organisms, such as mushrooms and toadstools, that do not have chlorophyll, so they cannot perform photosynthesis and make their own food. Fungi get the nutrients they need from living or dead plants and animals around them. Some fungi are considered parasites. Fungi reproduce through spores.

Q. WHAT ARE LICHENS?

A. Lichens are organisms created by the association of a fungus and an alga (plural: *algae*). The fungus supplies the alga with the water and mineral salts it needs for photosynthesis. The alga then performs photosynthesis and gives some of the nutrients it creates to the fungus. Lichens grow very slowly but can live as long as 4,500 years.

23

Ecosystems

➤ Tank Bromeliads can host a wealth of wildlife and form miniature ecosystems. These **aerial** plants grow on the branches and trunks of trees in the tropical forests of Central and South America. When rainwater collects inside their leaves, a tiny lake forms. This lake is soon inhabited by insects, frogs, and tiny crustaceans. Other animals, such as birds and snakes, also visit the plants to drink the water and feed on the small creatures that live there.

hummingbird

butterfly

vine snake

snail

dragonfly

tadpoles

tree frog

alligator lizard

Earth's tropical forests form some of the most important ecosystems. They are home to over half of the planet's animal and plant species. Tropical forest vegetation, or plant life, is divided into four layers: the emergent layer, which consists of the highest trees; the canopy, a thick layer of slightly lower trees; the shrub layer formed by woody, multibranched plants closer to the ground; and a ground layer of herbaceous plants.

Fascinating Facts

• The Amazon rain forest in Brazil is the largest tropical forest in the world. The Siberian Taiga is the largest nontropical forest. This immense woodland also contains wetlands where millions of water birds nest.

• Prairies are huge areas of grassland with few trees. The savanna in Africa and the Pampas in Argentina are different types of prairies.

Did you know?

Q. WHERE DO PLANTS LIVE?

A. Since they appeared on Earth, plants have slowly evolved to survive in all the different habitats on the planet, from dry deserts to swampy ponds and from cold polar regions to steamy tropical rain forests.

Q. WHAT IS AN ECOSYSTEM?

A. The physical environment of an area, including its air, soil, water, and weather, and the organisms that live in that environment, form an ecosystem. All the plants and animals in an ecosystem interact with one another and depend on one another for their survival.

Q. WHAT ARE THE MAIN THREATS TO EARTH'S ECOSYSTEMS?

A. Pollution and human destruction, such as the felling of huge areas of rain forest, are the main reasons why many ecosystems are disturbed or destroyed, and, as a result, many plants and animals are disappearing.

25

Unique Plants

The bushman's candle has a 4-inch (10-cm) stem that contains a peculiar substance. This waxy, fatty substance is flammable. When the plant's stem is set on fire, the bushman's candle burns unusually bright. This plant lives in the Kalahari Desert of Namibia, in Africa.

The titan arum is one of the smelliest plants! It produces a gigantic flower around 7 feet (2 m) high. The flower gives off a foul smell like rotting fish to attract pollinating insects. The plant grows in the tropical forests of Sumatra, Indonesia.

This species of *Mimosa* is very sensitive. At the slightest touch, the leaves of this plant close together along their stalks. After they close, it takes about half an hour for the leaves to uncurl and go back to their original positions. By rolling up, the plant protects itself from insect attacks.

▲ The flower of the mirror orchid looks like a female bee! The flower's appearance attracts male bees, which the plant needs to carry out pollination.

▼ The kapok tree has strong defenses. Its bark is covered with spikes that keep animals from reaching the leaves at the top of the plant. This large tree grows in tropical American forests.

Fascinating Facts

• The flowers of many plants open during the day, but night-scented stock only opens its flowers at night, since it is pollinated by nocturnal insects.

• *Acacia cornigera* has a special way of defending itself; it uses an army of ants! The ants live on the tree and sting any other insects that try to feed on the tree's leaves. The tree, in return, provides the ants with food and a place to live.

• To defend themselves, some plants mimic more dangerous plants. European *Lamiastrum galeobdolon* looks just like stinging nettle, so animals avoid it.

Did you know?

Q. HOW MANY SPECIES OF PLANTS ARE THERE IN THE WORLD?

A. Experts believe there are about 380,000 species of plants on Earth. Over thousands of years, these plants have adapted to many different environments.

Q. WHAT ADAPTATIONS HAVE PLANTS MADE?

A. Some plants have developed defense systems to protect themselves against attacks by animals. Flowering plants have developed special features to attract insects or other animals they need to carry out pollination.

Q. DO PLANTS COMPETE WITH EACH OTHER?

A. Plants compete with each other for the nutrients, sunlight, and water they need to survive. In the rain forest, for example, the vegetation is thick and often blocks out the Sun. In this environment, trees that can grow the fastest and reach the sunlight above the canopy first are the most likely trees to survive.

Q. WHAT IS BOTANY?

A. Botany is the study of plants, including everything from a plant's structure to how it interacts with other plants and animals to what diseases or parasites can harm a plant.

Q. WHEN DID PEOPLE START TO STUDY PLANTS?

A. The first people to study plants were the ancient Greeks. In the third century B.C., Aristotle, a famous Greek thinker, was the first to classify, or organize, plants. Later, in the first century B.C., Dioscorides, another Greek, recorded the descriptions of about 600 different plants, including information on their healing properties.

Q. WHO CREATED THE SCIENTIFIC CLASSIFICATION SYSTEM?

A. In the eighteenth century, Carolus Linnaeus, a Swedish botanist, classified many species of plants by giving each of them a genus name and a species name. Botanists all over the world are still using this scientific classification system to classify new plants they discover.

Records

➤ Sequoias, or redwoods, are the heaviest trees. These trees can tower to heights of 328 feet (100 m). One giant sequoia of California, called "General Sherman," weighs as much as 2,000 tons (1,814 metric tonnes). It is the heaviest living organism on Earth!

◀ Plants are very important for the survival of all living things, not only because they produce oxygen, but also because they are the first step in many food chains.

1. In the first step of this food chain, plants turn nonliving material, such as water and carbon dioxide, into food for themselves.

2. In the second step, plant-eating animals get nutrients from the plants.

4. In the final step of the chain, the meat-eating animal dies and its body is broken down by fungi, bacteria, worms, and other organisms. The animal's rotting body releases nonliving substances into the soil. Plants use these substances to make food, starting the food chain again.

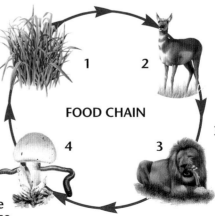

FOOD CHAIN

3. Meat-eating animals then feed on the plant-eaters.

◄ The banyan tree is one of the farthest reaching trees. Roots on this tropical tree grow down from its branches. When the roots reach the ground, they develop into rigid tree trunks that support the branches. Just one tree can have thousands of these roots, allowing the tree to grow long branches and stretch across a huge area.

Fascinating Facts

• Trees that grow in temperate areas, or areas that have distinct seasons, have a series of rings inside

their trunks. Each ring represents one season of growth, or one year in the life of the tree. Scientists can use these rings to tell how old a tree is.

• Bonsai is an ancient Japanese method of growing tiny trees. The plants are shaped with wires and pruned.

▼ Fossils of flowers not only show what flowers looked like millions of years ago, they also give scientists very important information about how flowering plants evolved.

► Raffia, a species of palm tree, has the largest leaves of any plant on Earth. Its leaves can measure up to 66 feet (20 m) in length. Raffia grows in Madagascar.

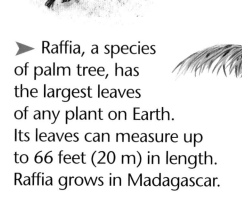

29

Glossary

adapted: changed or evolved to survive in a new environment.

aerial: growing in air instead of in soil.

cereal: a type of plant that produces a grain people use for food.

chlorophyll: a green substance produced by plants and used in photosynthesis.

deprive: take something away from or withhold something. A large tree, for example, can deprive the plants growing beneath it of sunlight.

diameter: the length of a straight line through the center of an object; an object's width through its center.

digest: break down food to absorb or remove the nutrients from it.

doses: the amounts or portions of medicine given or taken at one time.

environment: the surroundings in which plants, animals, and other organisms live.

evolved: changed or developed over a long period of time from one form to another.

germinate: begin to grow and develop; sprout.

habitats: places where a plant or animal naturally lives or grows.

host: the organism that a parasitic plant or animal depends on for food.

inflorescence: a cluster of flowers; the region on a plant where this cluster grows.

irritating: causing soreness; annoying.

microscopic: describing objects or organisms so tiny that a microscope is needed to see them.

nutrients: minerals and other matter an organism needs to survive and grow.

organisms: any living things.

parasite: a plant or animal that lives on or in another organism and depends on that organism for food.

photosynthesis: the process in which plants use sunlight to turn water and carbon dioxide into nutrients they need to survive.

pollen: tiny grains produced by the male organ of a plant.

pollination: the process in which pollen is carried from the male reproductive organs to the female reproductive organs in plants.

prey: an organism hunted by another organism for food.

primitive: of early times; not very evolved or simple in structure.

reproductive: relating to the ability to produce offspring.

scientific classification system: a system in which scientists organize plants and animals into related groups. The largest groups are kingdoms. Each kingdom is divided into classes, then orders, then families, then genera, and finally species. The paper birch tree, for example, belongs to the birch family and the *Betula* genus.

species: closely related animals or plants that are similar in behavior or appearance. Members of the same species can breed together.

textile: having to do with the making or selling of cloth.

wither: dry up; shrivel.

More Books to Read

Dig and Sow. How Do Plants Grow? Janice Lobb (Larousse Kingfisher Chambers)

The Environment. An Inside Look (series). Michael Allaby (Gareth Stevens)

Flowers. Eyewitness Explorers (series). David Burnie (DK Publishing)

Flowers, Trees, and Fruits. Young Discoverers: Biology Facts and Experiments (series). Sally Morgan (Kingfisher Books)

Forests. Under the Microscope (series). John Woodward (Gareth Stevens)

The Nature and Science of Plants. Exploring the Science of Nature (series). Jane Burton and Kim Taylor (Gareth Stevens)

Plants of Prey. Nature Close-Ups (series). Densey Clyne (Gareth Stevens)

The Science of Plants. Living Science (series). Jonathan Bocknek (Gareth Stevens)

Young Naturalist Field Guides (series). (Gareth Stevens)

Videos

Ecosystems: Nature in Balance. (AIMS Multimedia)

Flowers, Plants, and Trees. Tell Me Why (series). (Vision Quest Video)

Plant Life for Children (series). (Schlessinger)

Plants of the Rainforest. Rainforest for Children (series). (Schlessinger)

Web Sites

BrainPOP — Plant Animation
www.brainpop.com/science/plantsandanimals/

Plants of the Grasslands, Rain forest, Deserts, and More
mbgnet.mobot.org/sets/index.htm

Kid's Valley Garden
www.raw-connections.com/garden/

The Mysterious Venus Fly Trap
www.botany.org/bsa/misc/carn.html

Plants and Our Environment
tqjunior.thinkquest.org/3715/index.html

Some web sites stay current longer than others. For further web sites, use a search engine, such as www.yahooligans.com, to locate the following keywords: *angiosperm, flower, fungus, gymnosperm, photosynthesis, plants, pollination, rain forest, seaweed, seed, spore,* and *tree.*

Index

Acacia cornigera 27
alfalfa 12
algae 7, 22, 23
Alsomitra 10
angiosperms 6, 9

bacteria 7, 28
bald cypress 17
bamboos 12
bananas 11
banyan trees 29
baobabs 7
barley 13
beech trees 6
bladderworts 15
bonsai 29
botany 28
broad-leaf trees 6
bushman's candle 26

cattails 16
cereals 13
chlorophyll 7, 14, 22, 23
Clianthus 18
coconuts 10
conifers 6, 17
cotton 12
cypress 6

death cap mushrooms 23
deserts 18, 19, 26
dissemination 11
dodder 14
duck weed 17

elms 6
ephemeral plants 19
Euphorbias 19

ferns 20, 21
firs 6

fossils 29
foxgloves 13
fungi 22, 23

germination 11
giant puffball 22
giant rafflesia 8
Ginkgo biloba 6
gymnosperms 6

hemp 12
horsetails 20

Lamiastrum galeoobdolon 27
lichens 23
linen 12
Linnaeus, Carolus 28
Lithops 19
liverworts 20
luminous mushrooms 23

Madagascar periwinkle 12
magnolias 9
Mimosa 26
mirror orchid 27
mistletoe 14
mosses 20
mushrooms 22

night-scented stock 27

oaks 6
oats 13
orchids 8
ovaries 6, 9, 11
ovules 11

Pachypodium 18
palm trees 21, 29
papyrus 16
parasites 14, 15

parrot's bill 18
photosynthesis 7, 14, 19, 22, 23
phytoplankton 22
pines 6
pitcher plants 15
pollen 9
pollination 9, 27
pollution 25
Posidonia 16
pumpkins 10
Puya raimondii 9

raffia 29
redwoods 6, 28
rice 13
rye 13

Saguaro cactus 19
seaweed 22
sequoias 28
spores 6, 11, 20, 21, 23
stinging nettle 13, 27
stone plants 19
strangler fig 15
sundews 14
sunflowers 8

titan arum 26
toadstools 23
tropical forests 8, 24, 25, 26, 27
truffles 22

Venus fly trap 14
Victoria amazonica 17

water hyacinth 17
water lilies 16
Welwitschia 18
wheat 13